# The Black Girl's Guide to Building Wealth
## *A Personal Action Plan for Becoming Rich!*

LAKISHA RODWELL-GREEN

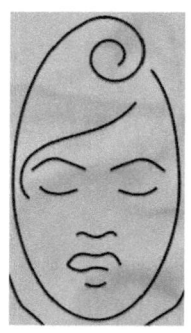

Copyright © 2016 Lakisha Rodwell-Green

All rights reserved.

ISBN: 153765344X
ISBN-13: 978-1537653440

## DEDICATION

This book is dedicated to women around the globe and our continued fight for justice, equality and a fair place in the world. Keep pushing.

# CONTENTS

**Introduction** — Page 7

Chapter One
***The Five Pillars of Success*** — Page 15

Chapter Two
***Why Black Girls Need a Wealth Plan*** — Page 25

Chapter Three
***A Snapshot of Black Wealth in America*** — Page 35

Chapter Four
***The Five Pillars of Wealth*** — Page 49

Chapter Five
***Strategic Steps to Building Wealth*** — Page 61

Chapter Six
***Habits to Grow Wealth*** — Page 97

**Afterward** — Page 113

**Appendix** — Page 115

## INTRODUCTION

Welcome to *The Black Girl's Guide to Building Wealth–A Personal Action Plan for Becoming Rich!* By selecting this book you've proved that you have already taken the crucial first step in building personal wealth. It is a tell-tale sign that your financial well-being is important to you. My goal with this book is to provide you with solid tools that lead to financial security and wealth.

Building personal wealth is an exciting journey, and I am thrilled and thankful that you've given me the opportunity to be a part of your journey. While building wealth is not always easy, it is often not as difficult as you may think. There will be stumbling blocks along the way, but you can and will get there with the help of the three P's–*patience, persistence,* and *positive thinking.*

This book comes out of my desire to share the knowledge I have learned in my own journey toward personal wealth. Along the way I've taken financial wrong turns that left me wondering whether I was going to pull through. These missteps did not ruin me financially. In fact, they were learning experiences that made me grow and get stronger. At times it was difficult to recover, but with a little faith and the help of my loved ones, I've been able to correct many of my financial mistakes. The ability to re-adjust and get back on track as quickly as I could has been the key to my personal financial growth.

Like so many others I have experienced a myriad of financial woes--poor credit, student-loan default, job loss, eviction, car re-possession. The list goes on. You name a financial mistake, and I've probably made it! During those times I never gave up on my goal of becoming wealthy. However, it always seemed as if some people were just good with money and that they must know something I didn't know. Then I realized that the only thing standing between me and my goal was knowledge.

Before I could turn my situation around, I had some serious soul-searching to do. I had to figure out why I always seemed to be piling on debt and moving farther away from the riches I desired. I had to admit that I did not understand my personal finances. I had been on my own for a long time, working to put myself through college and pay rent, but I had never learned the basics of personal finance. I had not learned the key financial skills of budgeting, saving, and investing. These three skills determine what we do with our money and what our money is then able to do for us.

Each of us works in some way to support ourselves and our families, but if we do not become familiar with the crucial skills of budgeting, saving, and investing, we will never get ahead financially. It won't matter how much money you make if you do not know how to properly spend, save, and invest your hard-earned money. Without these basics, working hard will not benefit you in the way that it should in building the lifestyle and legacy you want for yourself and your heirs. I used them to turn my financial situation around and so can you. You and your family should reap all the benefits possible from the hard work you put in at work and at home.

If you're like most people, you've likely had a financial "aha" moment. Maybe it was when you realized a co-worker was earning more money than you for doing the same job or perhaps when someone who earned less money than you seemed to have more to show for her money. These situations can often leave us feeling as if things are just not fair. We may begin to question why we are not getting the full value from our work, education, or efforts. These reactions are common and the confusion predictable. After all, women have enjoyed the possibility of exercising economic control over their lives for only a couple of generations, and many people still don't see the point in teaching a girl or young woman the basics of managing her financial affairs. Most of us have to learn the hard way, as I did.

This view may be a holdover from earlier times when we women often did not work outside the home and didn't need advice on investing because we didn't have any money of our own to invest. In the past, women often had to save a little of the money their husbands earned or pinch from the household budget just to afford a small purchase for themselves.

Historically, large numbers of Black women have always worked; often doing domestic work or child rearing for well to do families while still caring for their own families. Today, more than 60 percent of Black women are employed, a higher rate than either White or Hispanic women reach. Although Black women earn less than White men or White women, their earnings are highly correlated with educational level, and a third of employed Black women now have jobs in management or professional occupations.

We have come a long way and enjoy the freedom steady paychecks bring. Nowadays when Black women gather, there is usually no shortage of conversation about money—with an emphasis on spending money.

We may talk about going on vacation or buying a nice bag. Other times we may confide how much we paid for an item or share the terrific bargain we found. This type of fun and informative exchange is a way of sharing a great deal with our sisters. It may even be an opportunity for some friendly boasting to show that we can afford nice things. But just as our ability to earn money has evolved, our conversations around money can begin to evolve beyond spending.

My hope is that this book will spark rich conversations and information sharing about how we can earn more, save more and invest more of our hard earned money so that we are empowered to become wealthy. There is room for us to grow and change our conversations to focus not just on spending, but on *saving our money, building* assets, and *safeguarding our futures.*

When we save and invest our money, it begins to accumulate quickly through the power of a beautiful thing called compound interest. Compound interest literally multiplies money over time. Before we know it, with a few good habits, we can begin to accumulate real wealth. This wealth can then serve as a vehicle not only to take care of ourselves and our families, but to promote the kinds of change we want to see in our communities. Who among us does not want a beautiful home, nice cars, good schools, college educations for our children, and good-paying jobs for our loved ones?

Our communities face serious financial challenges, including high rates of unemployment and poverty. There is no magic wand that will erase poverty, blighted neighborhoods, or underperforming schools. There is also no government agency or political party that can solve these problems for us. They may help, but they cannot solve them. We are the keepers of our communities and we alone are responsible for us.

While we do face significant challenges in the Black community, our problems can change if we change. We can change our thinking and our habits to change our futures. With economic power we can create jobs, build homes and schools and help push our communities into prosperity.

The good news is it's never too early to begin saving and investing. In fact, the sooner we get started, the more wealth we can accumulate—and, of course, the more good we can do for ourselves, our families, and our communities. While reading, I encourage you to jot notes and questions you may want to follow up on or learn more about. A notes section is included at the end of the book. Let's get started.

## CHAPTER ONE
## THE FIVE PILLARS OF SUCCESS

When you think of success, what picture comes to mind? Do you think of expensive homes, nice cars, plenty of money in the bank? What about private schools for your children, extravagant vacations, designer clothes and shoes? If you answer yes, you would not be alone. These are often the things that drive us toward wanting to be successful and wealthy. While these are certainly outward signs of wealth and *financial* success, other important factors contribute to our notions of success as well. Think about the women you consider successful. Wealth is only one measure of what makes them successful. Take Michelle Obama, the first African American First Lady of the United States, for example. Prior to being First Lady, Mrs. Obama was successful in her own right.

Her accomplishments range broadly, from her education to her contributions to society. She graduated *cum laude* from Princeton with a degree in sociology and magnum cum laude from Harvard Law School with a Juris Doctorate degree. She married

Barack Obama while he was teaching constitutional law at the University of Chicago Law School, and she was practicing law at a well-known law firm in the city. She is the mother of two daughters: Malia (born 1998) and Natasha (Sasha born 2001). Over the course of her career—as a student, attorney, and then First Lady—she has dedicated her time and efforts to raising two beautiful daughters and to supporting initiatives and non-profit causes that benefit children and families.

    Although Mrs. Obama is wealthy, her wealth is not the sole measure of her success. She represents a successful African American woman because of her intelligence, style, grace, dedication to family, work on social initiatives as well as her candor. Although wealth may not be the only measure of success, it does, position us to promote the well-being of our families and have a positive impact on our communities. Underlying any successful community or society are five pillars: God, family, education, wealth and institutions. These five pillars are represented in the graphic below. Each pillar serves as the foundation for the next. For example, a belief in the basic family unit is grounded in some way in a belief in the Creator, whether God, Allah, Jehovah, or other Supreme Being(s). Similarly, a person or society cannot build wealth without first gaining education and knowledge. Without education or knowledge in the form of a skill there is no means to generate wealth. Let's take a closer look at each of the pillars of success.

**The Success Pyramid®**

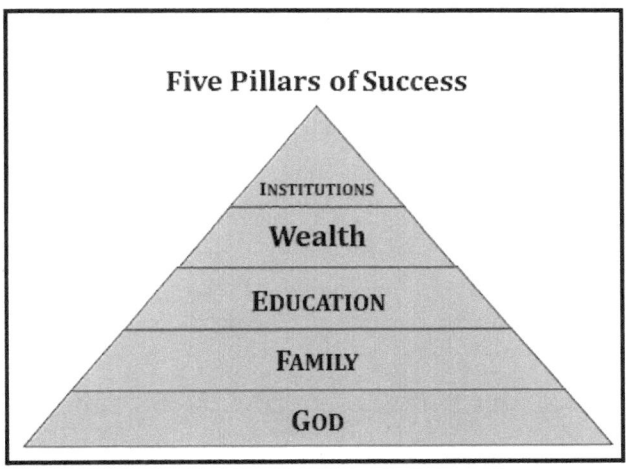

*The Success Pyramid represents the five pillars of success. These are the essential components of success in modern society.*

**The First Pillar: God**

The first success pillar is a belief in and relationship with the Creator in whatever manner you believe is appropriate for you and your family. This may include religious service, prayer, meditation, or other outward expressions of spirituality. This pillar of success may be the most important, because it provides us with the opportunity to practice faith. Faith plays a critical role in achieving success because it fosters the belief that we can accomplish our dreams and goals. The ability to accomplish anything in life begins with a notion that it is possible. Without believing in ourselves and having faith in a higher power, we would likely not believe we could achieve our goals.

**The Second Pillar: Family**

A stable family is an important factor in any plan for success because the family unit is one of the strongest social constructs in America. The family unit begins with the parents and extends to the children. Keeping the parental relationship intact is critical to the success of the family and for the children's well-being in particular. There are, of course, times when separation or divorce is in the best interest of the family, especially when spousal or child abuse is involved or one of the parents has neglected or jeopardized the mental or physical health of the spouse or the children. The financial stability of the entire family can also be put at risk by illegal activities (e.g., selling drugs) bad behaviors (e.g., using drugs) or chronic unemployment. The impact these activities exert on the family may need to be carefully considered and addressed if we truly want our family unit to be strong and capable of achieving financial success.

## The Third Pillar: Education

Education is important to financial success for many reasons, but I am going to focus on two key reasons. First, education has the largest influence on a person's lifetime earning potential. Therefore, a good formal education must be the primary goal for any young person in America. To put it another way, our ability to earn money is directly linked to our education. The more we learn, the more we will earn. Second, having a formal education is a great benefit if we decide to start a business and we will talk about the importance of business. We will discuss the importance of business ownership in the coming chapters

Moreover, formal education, training, and continued learning help us to become more actualized individuals. They drive us to realize our full potential, enabling us to become our best selves. In fact, American culture places such a high value on education, a person who has not graduated high school finds it difficult to develop fully into a functioning adult because of the challenges in finding sustainable employment without a high school diploma.

Investing in education for ourselves and our children begins with pre-school, continues through high school, and finishes with college or graduate school. Although formal education ends with college or graduate school, many successful individuals continue their learning and development throughout their lives, constantly discovering things that will improve their business, career, personal outlook and financial bottom line. Continuous learning is especially critical for us as women because we are often the first teachers of our children, and we want to be able to teach our children from a broad perspective of knowledge and understanding.

**The Fourth Pillar: Wealth**

The fourth pillar of success is wealth. It is important to distinguish wealth from income. Wealth represents a person's total financial outlook or the sum of all assets minus all debts. Said another way, our wealth is the total of what we *own* minus what we *owe* to others.

***The Wealth Equation:***

***Total Assets–Total Debt=Net Worth***

Having a good-paying job is a start to building wealth, but it's not enough. A person may have a high income and yet little accumulated wealth. On the other hand, another individual may not earn a large salary, but be able to build a substantial amount of wealth by living frugally and consistently saving over the years. We have all heard the stories about a regular person, who worked a regular job as, say, a librarian or school teacher who leaves an astonishingly large will on her death. The first time I heard a story like this I couldn't believe someone could save that much money in their lifetime.

Black women in particular are less likely to inherit a nest egg from our parents. We are also less likely to marry rich than our counterparts. Therefore, having a steady income that we can save and invest wisely will be the fastest path to building true wealth.

## The Fifth Pillar: Institutions

For the purpose of this book, we will define institutions as buildings and non-physical structures that are used to carry out the goals, ideals and values of a group of people or a society. Examples of institutions include schools, universities, libraries, hospitals, religious organizations and places of worship, banks, courts, media, police and military. One of the most pressing reasons for Black women to generate wealth is to leverage that wealth and begin creating these institutions for ourselves and for future generations. While we have many Black-owned churches, daycare centers, and even elementary schools, we are currently lacking in Black-owned hospitals, libraries, banks, and media. These are critical areas that we need to focus on strengthening, but that expansion will require substantial investment. We should keep these long term goals in mind as we develop our personal wealth. As we develop individual wealth, it can be pooled to create a strong economic base for Black Americans to exert the changes we'd like to see taking place in our communities. Let's explore further the value of us Black girls having wealth and what we hope to accomplish by building a strong wealth house for ourselves and our communities.

## CHAPTER TWO
## WHY BLACK GIRLS NEED A WEALTH PLAN

In the previous chapter we talked about the five pillars of success. In this chapter we explore the wealth pillar in more detail. The motivations behind the desire to build wealth are sometimes questioned. In fact, it's not uncommon for people to think that a person who focuses on becoming rich does so for selfish reasons or may be driven by personal greed. As a result, before we discuss *how* to acquire wealth; it's worth taking time to address *why* Black women need to acquire wealth.

If you think of a rich or wealthy person, what image comes to mind? Perhaps you picture a millionaire athlete or A-list entertainer driving a flashy car; living in a huge mansion; and jet-setting around the world on a private plane. Does this sound about right? Well, the image definitely represents some rich people, those with large incomes who spend a large proportion of their money and save and invest at a lower rate than one might expect, given their high income. This type of extravagant spending with limited saving and investment can lead to their "money running out" rather than their wealth growing over time. Individuals like these are not the best examples for us to follow if we are serious about becoming wealthy and staying wealthy.

A better choice for us would be the "quiet millionaires"— wealthy individuals or couples who have accumulated their wealth over time by consistent saving and investing. Very often the quiet millionaires are "regular" folks like business-owners or professionals working in law or medicine. In the 2008 HBO Comedy Special *Kill the Messenger*, the comedian Chris Rock famously joked that he lives in an exclusive community in Alpine, New Jersey. He points out that three other Black people live in this community—Mary J. Blige, Jay-Z, and Eddie Murphy. He goes on to explain this is interesting. While all of the Blacks in this exclusive neighborhood are mega-superstars, Rock's next-door neighbor who is White is a dentist. This comment says a lot and is actually not very far from the picture of race and wealth in America.

In the breakthrough book **The Millionaire Next Door: The Surprising Secrets of America's Wealthy**, *authors* Thomas J. Stanley and William D. Danko summarize years of their research on America's millionaires. Their findings challenge common assumptions about the rich. Stanley and Danko compiled volumes of data on millionaires; everything from how they gain wealth to how they save and spend their money. They found that the majority of millionaires they studied became wealthy by saving, being frugal, and learning to make smart investments.

In fact, many of the millionaires were either small business owners or professionals. Stanley and Danko paint a clear picture of the average millionaire. They live well below their means. They wear inexpensive clothing and drive American–made cars, many of them ten-years-old. They allocate their time, energy, and money efficiently, in ways conducive to building wealth. Almost all (97 percent) own their homes and the average value is $320K. Their average household net worth is $3.7 million, and they tend to be well-educated. Only one in five (20 percent) is not a college graduate, and many hold advanced degrees. Eighteen percent have master's degrees, and 6 percent have Ph.Ds. Most significantly, they are big investors. They invest nearly 20 percent of their household's realized income each year.

How does this picture of a "typical millionaire" compare to what you may have imagined?  If you're like most people, you will find the authors' description of the rich surprising.   It's important to note that the authors' focused their research on individuals with net worth in the $1 million to $10 million range.  They concentrated on this range specifically because this wealth range can typically be acquired in one generation, a critical point for us as African Americans.

Because of our unique history as descendants of American slaves, our ancestors were prohibited from earning money for their work for approximately 250 years or twelve generations.  Slavery legally ended with the Emancipation Proclamation in 1863 and subsequent passage of the Thirteen Amendment in December 1865. Although the Thirteenth Amendment freed African Americans and gave them the right to benefit from their work, they were largely uneducated and did not own property.  In addition, there were many laws on the books which impacted former slaves' freedom, constitutional rights and ability to earn money. Moreover, their family life had been horribly disrupted with family members sold off to other plantations with no way of maintaining communication with their loved ones.

After slavery ended, the practices of sharecropping and Jim Crow continued to prevent our ancestors from gaining access to decent education or to receive relatively equal compensation for their work. The circumstances surrounding our ancestors' entrance, presence, and purpose within American society place us as the descendants of American slaves in a uniquely underprivileged position compared to other members of American society, whose ancestors likely came to this country in search of financial opportunities or to express their religious, social and economic freedoms.

Since the end of slavery, African Americans have made substantial social and financial strides, despite the considerable inequalities and setbacks we have faced. Jim Crow and "separate but equal" laws, for example, stacked the deck against us in our ability to earn money and build wealth. As Black Girls, we are in the singular position of being both women and descendants of American slaves.

We know that women are typically paid less than their male counterparts for the same work. Within the family, women routinely assume the lion's share of caretaking for children and elderly family members. These two factors impact how much money a woman earns over the course of her lifetime. Black Girls, while we are doubly blessed with our blackness and our womaness, we absorb the financial impacts of both.

What does all of this mean? Well, it means that unless you are fortunate enough to have a trust fund waiting for you or you inherit money, you'll have to build your wealth from scratch. While it is no easy task to build wealth from nothing, it can be done. It requires a set of realistic wealth goals, creating a plan for achieving those goal, and working on your plan everyday. Yes, you heard me correctly. You have to work at building wealth everyday. That's the not-so-great news.

There is good news, however. These daily efforts do not have to be difficult to follow. It is certainly possible to become well-off with careful planning, saving, and investing, but certain levels of wealth are more easily reached than others. Wealth in the tens or hundreds of millions of dollars is referred to as generational wealth because this amount of wealth is seldom accumulated in one generation. For most of us, who come from humble means and will have to build our wealth from scratch, focusing on wealth accumulation in the $1 million to $10 million range is probably the most realistic and achievable wealth target.

Now that we have learned about the average American millionaire, it's time to turn our lens inward and focus on ourselves. What is it that we would like to have, do, and be when we reach our financial goals? What, for example, would your life be like if you were a millionaire?

## <u>Exercise 1</u>
### What would you do with $5 million dollars?

Sit back comfortably, close your eyes, and imagine that you have just won $5 million dollars in the lottery. Before you are able to process all of the great things you will be able to do with your winnings, however, you receive a telephone call from your doctor. She tells you that you have an incurable disease and have six months to live. As soon as you hang up the phone, you begin thinking about what you would like to do with your remaining time.

**Given the circumstances, what three things would you definitely want to accomplish in the time you have left?**

Write them down on a piece of paper as they come to mind. Do not think too long or hard on this. The idea is to write the first three things that come to mind.

## Exercise Review

Now let's review the three things on your list. What are they? Were you surprised by any of the things that came to mind first? Let's decode your answers. The $5 million dollars represents the idea that you do not have financial limitations to achieving your goals. Having six months to live represents a time pressure, or sense of urgency. The three things you chose to accomplish under these two circumstances represent your most pressing goals or desires right now. These are the goals that you should be working hard to achieve at the present time.

This exercise is meant to be a quick and easy way of filtering out things that are most important and urgent to accomplish with your money and your time. It's important to have a clear picture of why you want to become wealthy because it will serve as motivation for accomplishing your wealth goals. While some individuals may be motivated by a desire to take care of their family and give back to the community; others may want to lay a foundation for establishing generational wealth that can help to sustain their family through many generations.

One of my goals and a purpose of this book is to help strengthen my community by doing work that will help us to decrease and eventually eliminate the wealth disparity that exists between African Americans and other racial and ethnic groups. In the next chapter we'll take a look at this wealth disparity and try to generate ideas on ways to change it.

## CHAPTER THREE
## A SNAPSHOT OF BLACK WEALTH IN AMERICA

You'll recall from the previous chapter, our simplified measure of net worth is the value of our assets subtracting our debts. Just as it's possible to measure our individual wealth, it is also possible to measure the wealth of a larger group (a family, say, or a community). It would be nearly impossible to calculate the total of all assets owned by Black Americans. There are, however, several key wealth indicators that can be used to generate an overall picture of Black wealth in America. Understanding where Black Americans fit on the overall spectrum of wealth in America provides a useful starting point to quantify how much effort and work must be put in as individuals and as a group if we want to gain financial ground during the twenty-first century.

For our purpose, we will focus on eight wealth indicators: education, measured by the percentage of individuals earning a bachelor's degree or higher; income; marriage rate; home-ownership;

unemployment; poverty; business ownership; and household wealth. I've selected these indicators because they are the most significant factors we can control on an individual basis in trying to build personal and community wealth. Financially successful people typically have acquired a good education, own their homes, frequently operate their own businesses, have steady incomes, and have built household wealth. At the opposite end of the spectrum, the poorest members of our society tend to have lower rates of education, marriage, household and business ownership, and higher rates of unemployment.

Comparing the key wealth indicators for Black Americans to other racial and ethnic groups in America, we can begin to see why it is so important for us as Black women to build a strong financial house. In strengthening our personal financial lives, we strengthen our families and our communities.

## Wealth by the Numbers: Why Black Women Need a Personal Wealth Plan

| Wealth Indicator | Black Americans[+] | Hispanic Americans | White Americans | Asian Americans |
|---|---|---|---|---|
| Bachelor's Degree or Higher | 26% | 16% | 42% | 65% |
| Graduate Degree | 9% | 5% | 15% | 32% |
| Household Income | $35,000 | $37,000 | $54,000 | $66,000 |
| Marriage Rate | 36% | 51% | 57% | 60% |
| Home-Ownership | 45% | 48% | 71% | 59% |
| Home Value[#] | $81,000 | $105,000* | $123,000 | $199,000 |
| Unemployment Rate (1Q 2016) | 8% | 4% | 5% | 3% |
| Poverty Rate | 26% | 23% | 10% | 12% |
| Business Ownership | 5% | 8% | 11% | 11% |
| Median Household Wealth | $11,184 | $13,900 | $134,008 | $91,440 |

Source: US Census Data 2010-2104 unless noted

+Data include males and females

#Source: US Census Data 2000

*Denotes overlap with other racial categories.

## **Education**

Education is the single most important factor in determining a person's lifetime earning potential. Both the education level and type of education obtained have a critical impact on one's earnings. A recent study of income and education shows the average estimated lifetime earnings for those with a high school diploma is $1.2 million compared to $2.1 million for those earning a bachelor's degree. A master's degree yields an average of $2.5 million in lifetime earnings while doctoral and professional degrees net $3.4 million and $4.4 million respectively.

Based on data gathered during the 2010 Census, approximately 26 percent of Black Americans had attained a bachelor's degree or higher, compared to 42 percent of Whites and 65 percent of Asians. Only 9 percent of Black Americans had earned a graduate degree, approximately two-thirds the rate of White Americans (15 percent) and less than one-third the rate of Asian Americans (32 percent).

## Income

Income level is closely tied to the ability to generate wealth. There are, however, two different kinds of income: earned income, which comes from salaries, and unearned income, in the form of interest, dividends, and short- and long-term capital gains. When, however, a person is just starting out and building wealth from scratch, employment income is often the only source of money available to build wealth.

The more she earns, the faster and easier it becomes for her to generate wealth. As income increases, the cost of basic needs like food, clothing, housing, transportation, and education do not increase proportionately. As a result, she will have more disposable income for saving and investing in income-producing assets and investments like real estate, stocks, mutual funds, and businesses. Over time, the investment income can surpass employment income as the main source of wealth. This is one way the rich continue to get richer. When passive income reaches a sizable portion of the total income coming into the household, a family's wealth begins to accumulate at a *much* faster rate.

At the time of the 2010 census, Black Americans earned less income per year than all other major racial groups in America: $35,000 per year compared to $37,000 annually for Hispanics, $54,000 for Whites, and $66,000 per year for Asians. If we want to get ahead financially increasing our annual household income will need to be a top priority of our financial plans.

## **Marriage**

African Americans, unlike other ethnic or racial groups in America, have a singular history with respect to rates of marriage. During slavery our ancestors were forbidden to marry. However, by the first half of the twentieth century, Black women and men married in roughly equal rates to Whites. After the 1950's marriage rates declined for all races, however the decline in rate was most significant for Black women. In 1950 the marriage rate was approximately the same for Black women and White women, 67 percent and 64 percent respectively. However by 1998 the percentage of married White women dropped to 58 percent (a 13 percent drop) however the percentage of married Black women was 36 percent (a 44 percent drop).

There are surely a myriad of reasons for this sharp decline. Two key factors may be the high rates of unemployment and incarceration among African Americans, our men in particular. While African Americans make up 13 percent of the American population, they make up 35 percent of all inmates and, as of 2014, 37 percent of the 2.2 million male inmates.[1] This high rate of incarceration and unemployment undoubtedly has an impact on the available pool of eligible African American men.

Marriage rates tend to be lower among those individuals living in poverty while the majority of millionaires and billionaires are married. Marriage impacts income and wealth accumulation in several ways. Examples of the financial benefits of marriage are the tax advantages of filing joint tax returns, shared living expenses, shared health insurance benefits and the possibility of receiving a spouse's pension, social security income, or other retirement

---

[1] Prison Inmates at Mid-Year 2014, U. S. Department of Justice.

benefits. Because women typically earn less than men, marrying may have a larger financial benefit for a woman than for her husband. Some of the financial risks of marriage include shared financial responsibility for debts in certain cases, and the possibility of paying more taxes if married filing jointly, especially in the case of two high earning individuals.

## **Homeownership and Home Value**

Black Americans own fewer homes than our White, Hispanic and Asian counterparts. Only 45 percent of Black Americans own a home compared to 48 percent of Hispanic Americans, 59 percent of Asian Americans and 71 percent of White Americans. For many reasons homeownership is a critical step in building wealth. First, the mortgage payment is the largest household expense, and homeownership offers significant tax breaks, including the ability to deduct mortgage interest payments, insurance, and real estate taxes. These tax deductions can represent a substantial savings each year, but only if you own the home you live in. If you rent, you do not get to claim these deductions. In addition, if you run a business out of your home, you may claim certain other deductions as well.

Arguably, the most important reason for owning a home is that homeownership offers a sense of security and permanence that you simply do not have when renting. This sense of security stems, in part, from the historical appreciation in home values. Typically a higher home value leads to greater wealth as the equity in your home builds, and for most Americans a majority of their wealth is tied to the value of their home. This is why so many Americans lost a significant portion of their wealth during the housing crash of 2008.

The housing crash, however, is an exception to the historical pattern of appreciation. In 2000 the median home value for Black Americans was $81,000 compared to $105,000 for Hispanics, $123,000 for Whites and $199,000 for Asians. These numbers are based on data from the 2000 Census. We are using the 2000 Census data as a comparison because the 2010 housing data would be heavily impacted by the housing bubble and subsequent crash. The aftershocks of the crash lasted from approximately

2002 through 2008 and affected Black Americans disproportionately. Predatory lending practice leading to the crash exposed more Black Americans to adjustable rate mortgages rather than fixed rate mortgages and resulted in widespread foreclosures.

## **Unemployment and Business Ownership**

During the first quarter of 2016 the officially reported unemployment rate for Black Americans was 8 percent compared to 4 percent for Hispanics, 5 percent for Whites, and 3 percent for Asians. Many speculate the unemployment rate for Black Americans may be higher than reported. We do not have the time or space in this short book to go into detail on all the different reasons why our unemployment rates are double and almost triple that of other races, but one key factor worth discussing is the low rate of business ownership among Black Americans.

There is a link between the unemployment rate and business ownership rate. According to a recent article in Forbes magazine small businesses have generated over 65% of the net new jobs since 1995. And yet, a community that does not create jobs cannot employ members of their community. Black

Americans have lower rates of business ownership and higher rates of unemployment than other groups.

Driving or walking through many of our communities during the day, we see large numbers of working-age adults in the neighborhood rather than working at a job, operating their own business, or attending school. If we take a moment to think about the working-age members of our own community, how many can we count who are unemployed? What about those who are under-employed or working at a job for which they are over-qualified?

Business ownership rates are 5 percent for Blacks, compared to 8 percent for Hispanics, and 11 percent for Whites and Asians. Now let's think about this for a moment. When we patronize small businesses owned by Asians, Whites or Hispanics, we usually see Asians, White or Hispanics respectively working there. It is unrealistic to think that African Americans should not focus on entrepreneurship as much as other ethnic groups. If we are to have jobs we must create jobs, and that is only done through entrepreneurship. It would be silly to believe that non-Black business owners will employ large numbers of Black employees simply out of the kindness of the heart. And yet if we are not actively starting businesses and patronizing businesses, how will we decrease the unemployment disparity? How often are we going out of our way to patronize the Black-owned businesses in our communities? What Black owned businesses exists in our communities?

Here's a little quiz. Excluding hair salons and barbershops, can you name five Black-owned businesses in your city or town? Other races of people are creating jobs and employing people. We must do the same to survive and prosper financially. We can only employ others if we own businesses. Later in the book we will discuss the importance of entrepreneurship and owning a business no matter what your professional background.

## **Poverty**

As of the 2010 Census, over a quarter of Black Americans live in poverty. This is a heart-wrenching statistic, but it speaks to the urgent need for us to work as hard as possible to secure our financial future for ourselves, our families, and our communities. This goal has to be a top priority for us. And it must be something that we work hard at each and every day. Focusing on our finances, earning, saving and investing money are things we must do each and every day. There are simple ways to do this. It is not enough to think about money only when a financial emergency or crisis hits. We have to work proactively on finances, building a little at a time and being as consistent as possible.

## **Household Wealth**

A review of the 2010 Census data for household wealth uncovers staggering figures. On average, an Asian American family has eight times the wealth and a White family has eleven times the wealth of a Black family. This is a heavy reality to face and yet if we do not face it soon, I fear the situation will only get worse over time, not better. We have to begin taking a long, hard look at our habits and behaviors and to understand the impact of our choices. Over the long term good financial habits lead to wealth and poor financial habits lead to poverty.

Our lack of wealth should be a topic of daily conversation for us. We should be thinking about and talking about how to improve our financial standing every day with our spouses, children, girlfriends, parents, and neighbors. After all, don't we all do some amount of work every day? When was the last time you did absolutely no work at all for an entire day? As women we rarely get a day completely free from work.

The work that we do is so commonplace, it can easily go unnoticed: work for our jobs, housework, homework, school work, paperwork, doing hair, doing laundry, running errands, checking on and caring for our elderly and sick loved ones and neighbors. Just thinking about all this work is enough to make a person tired.

We have to eat to live, and work to eat. And I don't see anyone offering to feed us; therefore, we have to do it ourselves. It follows that if we are working every day, we should be thinking about the fruits of our labor every day—not only how to spend our money but also how to increase our earnings to support the lifestyle and future we want for our families and future generations. The next chapter will begin to tell us how to just that.

## CHAPTER FOUR
## THE FIVE PILLARS OF WEALTH

There are an unlimited number of ways to earn income, and fortunately America has a capitalist, free-market economy, with comparatively few restrictions on earning income. The U.S. economy is considered capitalist because individuals can produce, own and control property, businesses, and other assets as opposed to a communist system under which the government owns or heavily controls property and assets. As a free-market economy, the U.S. government does not fix prices of goods and services or impose heavy regulations, with some exceptions on what people can and cannot buy. Rather, the laws of supply and demand determine the cost and quantity of goods and services produced.

Common sources of income include employment, businesses, and investments such as stocks, bonds, and real estate. Grouping our income into categories is a useful tool in creating a personal wealth plan, which we will discuss shortly, but first let's review some basic tenets or building blocks of wealth.

## The Wealth Equation:
### *Total Assets-Total Debt=Net Worth*

In chapter one, we discussed the wealth equation, which states a person's net worth is the value of assets owned minus what is owed. If we want to increase our net worth, we must increase our assets and lower our debt. This sounds simple enough, but how do we go about doing this when we may be starting from nothing?

Honestly, getting started with no money is probably the most challenging part of building wealth. Building wealth starting with no nest egg is like trying to pedal a bicycle uphill. It will not happen unless you approach it in a specific way. You cannot start pedaling uphill from a seated position. You need momentum to get the bike to take off. Building wealth is the same. We must gather momentum in the form of income, savings, and investments to help get our wealth off the ground. Contrary to what we are taught while growing up, or exposed to in the media, getting rich is not a matter of luck. Rather it requires a set of skills, and it's important to use the correct skills to get the job done.

Let's begin with a simple premise: Our wealth is similar to a house. Like any house, our wealth house is built on a foundation. We know that a home with a strong foundation made of stone or brick will stand the test of time unlike a house built with shoddy materials. Similarly we want to make sure we build our wealth house on a solid foundation of good assets. You may be wondering, "What are assets"? We've mentioned the word a few times so far, but what exactly is an asset? In a financial sense, an asset is anything that you own that has value. An asset can be any type of personal property, such as the home, car, furniture, jewelry, or artwork you own. If you do not own your home outright, you can consider the equity you've accumulated. When calculating your net worth; you must deduct any debts owed on the property from its fair-market value to get at the real equity. The same goes for your car or other personal property.

Assets also include investments such as stocks, bonds, mutual funds, and retirement accounts as well as savings accounts, checking accounts, money-market accounts, and certificates of deposit (CDs). Finally, a business can be a great asset because it has unique advantages, such as tax advantages and the ability to employ workers who then benefit from the business as well. For our purposes, we will focus on three asset categories: investments, real estate, and businesses. These three asset types combined with employment income and insurance of any kind make up our wealth house. Just as there are five pillars of success, there are five pillars of wealth.

## **The Five Pillars of Wealth**

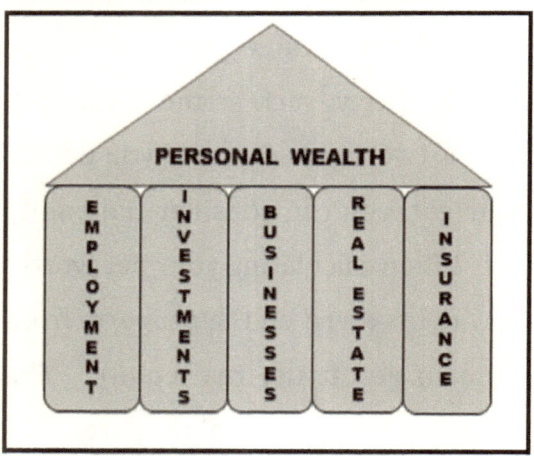

**The Five Pillars of Wealth represent three types of assets and employment and business income**

The wealth pillars are equal in height and width to demonstrate they are equally important in creating and fortifying personal wealth. While most of us have employment income and maybe even one or two of the other wealth pillars, it can be challenging to accumulate all five. In chapter five we will talk about ways to build each of these wealth pillars from the ground up. For now let's review each of the wealth pillars and what they mean.

## **Employment Income**

Employment income is a key source of revenue, and for most of us, responsible for most of our income. We have to work to survive, as James Brown famously said, *"If you don't work, then you can't eat."* Securing employment income is the first step in building wealth from scratch. Even if your goal is to be an entrepreneur and work for yourself, getting a job first will help you to learn valuable skills that you can apply in operating your own business.

Although employment income is the first pillar of wealth, there are limitations with regards to employment income that do not exist with the other types of income and assets in the wealth house. First, employment income depends on the availability of a job.  That means, the business owner must create the job and keep it open so that you can work there.  Second, employment income is limited by time, because a person can only work a limited number of hours in a day, typically no more than eight hours per day or forty hours per week.  Even with overtime or a second job, the income is still bound by the number of hours you can physically work.  Finally, employment income is limited by the individual's physical and mental ability to work.  A personal injury or illness that limits our ability to work, limits our employment income, which can be a blow to our finances.

**Investment Income**

Examples of investments include stocks, bond, mutual funds, and real estate.  Investments generate income in the form of interest or dividends (in the case of stocks).  Investment income does not have the limitations that employment income has.  This is the reason investments are critical to building real wealth.  Interest and dividends earned from stocks, bonds, or mutual funds tend to grow over the long-term and are not limited by the amount of time in a day as employment income is. In fact, with investment income you can make money twenty-four hours a day, and time works to your benefit. The sooner you invest, the more money you can make on these investments over the long-term.

## Insurance

There are many types of insurance and some are designed for specific needs. Most, however, work in a similar way. Their purpose is to protect a person against loss of money or property. Insurance provides a guarantee that in the event of a loss or unexpected expense, the individual will receive payment or have certain services paid (for example, medical procedures covered by health insurance). The most common types of insurance include life insurance, health insurance, auto insurance, home insurance, disability insurance, unemployment insurance, accident insurance, and rental insurance.

Insurance is an important part of any wealth plan because it enables protection of our assets and property. Insurance coverage such as disability and life insurance serves to protect us and our families against lost income due to injury or death. Disability insurance protects in the event that you are hurt and cannot work. This can be one of the most important types of insurance to carry. If you are offered disability insurance through work take advantage of this benefit. You may have a few options of premium and payout amounts. This is a benefit you may want to consider maxing out. Often the difference in the premium is minimal (maybe a few dollars per paycheck), but if you need to go on short-term or long-term disability leave, the difference in disability pay may be significant.

I'll give a personal example of this; one of my previous jobs offered two disability options for 40 percent or 66 percent of gross salary. While the difference in premium cost was only a few dollars per pay check, the 66 percent option paid substantially more money. In this example if you earn $40,000 per year, your weekly pre-tax pay rate is $729. The disability pay at 40 percent would be $307 per week compared to $481 per week for the 66 percent option. That is a significant difference in payment. In this example for a disability lasting six weeks the difference is $1,044.

Life insurance protects a person's heirs and beneficiaries by providing money that would be used to replace lost income in the event of death. This is another important type of insurance to hold especially for those with children or a spouse to provide for. Whatever expenses you want to ensure payment of in the event of your death are calculated in the life insurance amount you choose. For example, if you would want your spouse to be able to pay off the mortgage on the family home and pay for the children's college education, these expenses should be factored into the decision on how much life insurance coverage to carry. Another example is if you have a disabled child who is unable to work. You may want to factor in the cost of the expenses of her care as well.

It is important to speak with a qualified and knowledgeable insurance broker or agent regarding your specific insurance needs, as insurance remains an important way to protect our assets from loss. Because loss of an income stream or loss of property can have a significant financial impact on you and your family, it is critical to be properly insured to protect your assets to enable your family to continue building wealth.

To drive home the importance of insurance think about taking out a bank loan to purchase a car or a home. The bank requires you to carry enough insurance on the vehicle or the home to cover the loss of property. You cannot drive your car off the lot or take ownership of your home before providing proof of insurance. The bank will not take the risk of having uninsured property and neither should you.

## **Real Estate**

Real estate consists of land and any property on the land. Real Estate is a key factor in building wealth for several reasons. Home-ownership enables the home-owner to build equity (ownership) at the same time that it provides shelter. With each mortgage payment made, we can build equity in the home so that once the bank note is paid off; the home is owned outright. Property is also an important piece of the wealth puzzle because we can earn passive income by renting the land or property. Finally, because land is a finite resource, land and property values tend to appreciate over time. This does not mean that property values never decrease or that you cannot lose money on real estate; however, it is likely that a sound real-estate purchase today will continue to appreciate over the long term.

## Business Ownership

Owning a business is the ultimate way of generating passive income. Unlike the salary made working at a job, income earned from a business is not limited to the time you personally have available to work. A business can earn as much money as there are potential customers; therefore, the possibilities for income are limitless. A business can employ two employees or two thousand. The jobs that are performed by the employees make the business money. In return, the business provides employment and salaries to its employees. As mentioned, one of the key benefits of business ownership is the ability to create jobs and employ members of our community.

This is not as hard as it may sound. For example, if you own and operated a childcare center from your home and you have the ability to hire someone to assist you in caring for the children, you have created a job. If you bake cakes and sell them to local business, you may have the ability to create a job for someone to make the deliveries.  If you are a hair dresser and you employ a shampoo girl, you have created a job.  The ability to create jobs is a powerful benefit of business ownership and has a tremendous impact on our community.  Most important for your business, hiring someone to do some small part of the duties will free up your time to take on bigger tasks—for example, landing more clients or changing the pricing policy to increase the bottom line.

Now that we've learned the many ways to generate income, let's turn our attention to specific strategies to use income to build a nest egg.

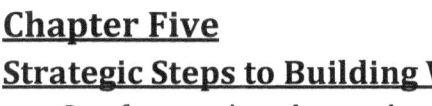

# Chapter Five
## Strategic Steps to Building Wealth

So far, we've learned about five pillars of success, five pillars of wealth, wealth indicators, the state of Black wealth in America, and reasons for having a wealth plan. In this chapter we focus on a strategy to accumulate wealth and the action steps you can implement to get where you want to be financially. Any plan for accumulating wealth is built from at least three elements: earning, saving, and investing. Once you've set your goals and created your personal financial plan, however, it will take some discipline to follow the action steps. Listed below are strategic steps you should consider to implement your plan for wealth accumulation. If you have already taken some of these steps good for you! You're off to a good start. In that case move on to implementing the next step.

### *Strategic Step No.1: Invest in Education*

As we pointed out earlier, education is the single most important factor in determining a person's lifetime earning potential. The average estimated lifetime wage is $1.2 million for a high school diploma,

$2.1 million for a bachelor's degree, and $2.5 million for a master's degree, $3.4 million for a Ph.D. and $4.4 million for a medicine or law degree. Now that is a substantial amount of coin! Take a moment to think about what the difference in earnings would mean in terms of everyday life. Compared to a high school diploma, earning a bachelor's degree essentially doubles the value of the home you can buy, the value of the car you can drive, and the amount of money you have to save and invest. The three- or fourfold increase of a doctoral or professional degree would make a remarkable difference to the lifestyle choices available to you.

Getting an education is a process, but may not be as hard as you may think. And it is clearly an investment that continues to pay off over the course of a lifetime. One of the toughest parts may be just in getting started. In the case of post-secondary education, getting started involves deciding what you will study.

One recommendation is that you first determine what you are naturally interested in and good at doing. Then research the different college majors available to you and the careers that graduates in these fields pursue. Try to uncover basic and practical information, such as how much individuals working a particular field earn. With a general idea of the salaries in a particular field, you can dig deeper:. are jobs plentiful or restricted to a niche industry? What does the long-term career path look like? What options are available to continue my education in this field? What is the difference in salary for a bachelor's degree or master's degree in this particular field?

A recent study performed by the Hamilton Project, *Major Decisions: What Graduates Earn Over Their Lifetimes*, looked at median earnings for eighty college majors. The study found majors emphasizing quantitative skills, such as engineering, computer science, operations and logistics, physics, economics, and finance, tended to have graduates with the highest lifetime earnings. Majors that focused on working with children and providing counseling services tended to produce the lowest earnings. The lowest paying fields include early-childhood education, family sciences (home economics), theology, fine arts, social work, and elementary education.

According to the report engineering majors topped the list of highest earners and engineers tended to be wealthier than other college graduates. One theory is that the analytical skills developed in engineering tend to help with financial decision making. It is worth taking some time to read this report and to do additional research and due diligence before selecting a college major. Parents can also provide their high-school-age children with this type of information to help them in their selection of college majors. Carefully researching and selecting a college major is an important step in securing a well-paying job in the future.

If you are a mature woman who is well into your work career, you may want to weigh the options of advancing in your current career compared to changing paths. Consider whether your experience can be leveraged for a higher paying job in your current field. Will your current employer pay for you to return to school? Will you be able to enter a new field at or close to your current salary level? Some jobs will compensate you for years of experience worked in a different field. Many employers encourage continuing education for their employees and offer college tuition reimbursement for those who want to return to school. If you are in this situation, check into the opportunities that exist with your employer. For those who are employed by a university or college, often the cost to attend the school is waived. This is an excellent benefit to take advantage of.

If you are already working in your chosen career or profession, consider ways to boost your pay grade with additional education and training. How much more, for example, would a master's degree add to your paycheck for doing the same job? Would you qualify for a more senior position in your current field by earning a master's degree or Ph.D.? Would additional education or training qualify you to earn extra income by consulting, teaching, or writing? Online learning and for-profit universities have increased the demand for teachers in many fields of study. Consider if you would be able to leverage your education and experience into a teaching position.

Those who dream of being an entrepreneur may think you do not need an education to become a business owner. This perception couldn't be farther from the truth. An education is still a good investment because the knowledge and skills learned in college are transferable. These skills improve your business acumen and the prospects for success of any entrepreneurial venture you undertake. Employers often pay for their employees to return to school because they realize the benefits of an educated employee. Education helps provide a broader understanding and sharpens your skill set as an employee; it will do the same for you as a business owner.

When beginning a business, you have to understand all facets of the business. Initially you will be an army of one–responsible for conducting the core business function as well as the advertising, finance, sales, marketing, bookkeeping and purchasing. Your education also enables you to work in your chosen field of study until the business generates enough income to get off the ground and pay your full salary.

***Strategic Step No. 2: Get Started Now!***

Making a financial plan can be intimidating to even the smartest individuals and there may be a tendency to want to put it off. We may feel that we'll know more about finances in the future and be better prepared to make important financial decisions later in life. The truth is that we have to start somewhere, and the best way to know more in the future is to begin learning *now*. It's also important to begin saving and investing for your future immediately because time is a critical element in accumulating wealth. Wealth is not built in a day. *Real wealth* is built over time by implementing consistent habits and practices. The following examples will illustrate why time is essential.

While it is not a secret that many lottery winners end up broke, it is interesting to understand why this happens. Can you imagine what it would feel like to win the lottery only to end up bankrupt within a few years? It must be devastating to have so much money in hand and somehow let it slip through your fingers like grains of sand. This type of loss is not unique to lottery winners. In fact, professional athletes also have a high likelihood of ending up broke. A study conducted by *Sports Illustrated* found that between seventy-five and eighty percent of professional athletes ended up broke within two to five years of retirement.

What could make a person who comes into millions of dollars go broke so quickly? Part of the challenge that both lottery winners and professional athletes face is that they come into their wealth quickly. In many cases they go from having very little money to being instant millionaires. Yet they have not had an opportunity to learn about money and finances. It is the equivalent of turning over car keys to a person who has not learned to drive. Almost overnight this (typically) young person has access to large amounts of money and little understanding of how to make their money last, let alone make it grow over time. I believe coming into a large sum of money from having very little also gives a skewed view of the windfall. Ten or even twenty million dollars may be a lot of money, but it won't last long if you are trying to support your entire extended family in a lavish lifestyle.

Moreover, the athlete or lottery winner is probably the richest person in his or her family or social circle and may have no friends or family members with solid financial knowledge to turn to for guidance on saving and investing   And finally it may also be a case of "give a man a fish and he'll eat for a day, but teach him how to fish and he'll eat forever." Buying possessions for loved ones may not be the best gift to give. Instead, paying for a loved one's education or matching their own savings may be a better option to help them survive and thrive financially over time.

This discussion is not meant as a condemnation of athletes or any other individuals who try to take care of their loved ones. Rather stating there are other alternatives that may put the successful individual in a position to leverage their wealth in ways that will strengthen and support their family for generations to come.

Contrast a lottery winner's instant wealth with a woman who builds wealth over time. Creating wealth over time gives her hands-on experience saving and investing her own money. She builds confidence in her financial decision-making skills as she comes to understand the wealth-building techniques that have worked well. Just as importantly, she will recognize what has not worked and how to avoid making the same financial mistakes repeatedly. Earning her money over time, she values and appreciates it more.

She will value each hard earned dollar because she realizes how long it has taken to earn.

Many parents work hard to provide for their children, but neglect to teach them the value of money or basic financial management. As a result, the children grow up accustomed to being well-off; yet do not understand the sacrifices their parents made to accumulate wealth. It is not uncommon for the parents' financial legacy to be lost within one generation. There is a saying among the well-off, "from shirtsleeves to shirtsleeves in one generation." In other words, an entire fortune can be lost in one generation if it is not properly protected.

Building wealth over time provides an opportunity to adjust gradually to the many changes and challenges that accompany wealth. Like a garden, money requires cultivating. And just as gardening takes time and trial and error, learning to protect and cultivate our money requires similar time and effort. Therefore it is critical to begin earning, saving, and investing your money right away. The sooner we begin saving and investing the longer we have to grow our money and the more time we have to educate ourselves about how to protect our wealth.

Although it is ideal to begin your financial education early in life, it is never too late to begin learning about finances. It is better to learn about money later in life than never at all. Regardless of your age, experience or educational background, anyone can gain financial education. The sooner we begin, the more wealth we can accumulate during our lifetime and the more time we have to teach others including our children, grandchildren, spouse, siblings and friends. The next strategic step will show you how to free up extra money to begin saving.

## Strategic Step No. 3: Create a Budget, to Spend Less and Save More

There is a saying "It's not what you make, it's what you keep." I definitely believe this is true. We all know individuals who just seem to be naturally good with money. No matter what their salary or earnings may be, they seem to have a lot to show for it. They are generally good at saving and putting money away for a rainy day and they always seem to have money available when they need it. They don't run out of money or live paycheck to paycheck as so many do.

The ability to save is indeed a valuable skill to learn. I call it a skill because it requires discipline and attention. Although some individuals may have a natural inclination to spend less and save more, it takes a great deal of discipline and practice for many of us. Saving money is not something we are naturally born knowing how to do, and unfortunately American culture currently places a higher value on consumer spending and acquiring credit than on saving and living a frugal lifestyle. This was not always the case.

In fact, over the last several decades there has been a shift in how people view money and spending, but little has changed in the way that we earn our money. Previously there was a greater focus on spending modestly and having minimal credit obligations. In days past it was a common aim to work to own a home and a car outright and to have minimal, if any, credit obligations. This ideal has been replaced by a desire to have more and bigger material possessions. It has become pretty common practice to purchase a starter home and use the built-up equity to upgrade to a larger home. Summer vacations to visit family "down south" have been replaced by family cruises and trips to the Caribbean. These changes represent a newer way of thinking and there is nothing wrong with this desire to go bigger and better! In fact it is a good thing to dream big and work towards the things we want in life. We just have to mind our dollars to make sure that we are planning and able to afford larger purchases in time and definitely not putting a financial burden on ourselves to live above our means.

Another recent change is a larger media and government focus on business and the financial state of the business sector compared to the financial well-being of the people. While high consumer spending greatly benefits businesses and the economy in some ways, overspending is never good for the individual.

Avoiding overspending can be done by using a budget. Creating a budget allows you to plan your spending. I recommend a monthly budget based on your *gross* salary (not net) and all other forms of income. Include all deductions from your pay into your budget including taxes, health insurance, 401k deductions, and disability insurance. If you receive any other form of income, you want to make sure you include this money as well, for example if you receive child support alimony, or a disability payment, include this amount in your overall monthly income. Next you want to calculate what percentage of your total income each expense accounts for. Include taxes, healthcare and 401K deductions along with utilities, food, clothing, everything you spend money on in a month, should be included. This monthly budget based on gross income will show at a glance exactly where the money is going. Remember it is important to track every expense and to be honest about what you are spending.

Once you've created a realistic budget you'll likely see immediate areas to cut costs. A few of the common areas where expenses may be larger than you realize are taxes, entertainment, cell phone, cable, dining out and grooming expenses such hair styling, manicures and pedicures. The following strategic steps will help you begin earning and saving more money.

***Strategic Step No. 4: Secure the Highest Paying Job You Can Get Today and Start Saving for Retirement***

Increasing your salary is a critical step in gaining more money to save and invest. If you are still in school, a higher paying job allows you to begin earning more money now. Earning a higher salary, gives you access to more money to begin saving and investing. If you are already working while getting your education, explore whether there is another type of job available to you that would pay more money. For instance, if you worked at a fast-food restaurant in high school, and are now enrolled in a community college or a university, you have some additional education you didn't have when you began in your position. You may be able to leverage these additional months or years of education into a higher paying job at another company or into a higher salary in your current job.

Does your boss know that you are working toward a degree? Sometimes the only thing standing between us and a pay raise is asking for it. Women are less likely than men to negotiate a higher starting salary or pay raise than men. The truth is it never hurts to ask, the worst they can say is no. Also explore other options for increasing your salary, such as finding a similar job with another company. You are more likely to get your asking pay rate at the initial negotiations. Some people mistakenly think they will work a little to prove themselves before negotiating more money, don't make this mistake. Ask for what you want up front before you've agreed to take the job, and you're more likely to get it.

If you are a full-time college student, one way to increase your pay is to get an off-campus job. Business owners like to hire college students because they view them as being motivated and willing to learn. These are qualities that business owners and managers value in an employee.

In some instances, it may be preferable to delay working until after you have graduated. It is difficult, for example, to hold a part-time job while earning a medical or law degree. Similarly, if you are a young woman with no children and no other financial responsibilities, you may be able to take more classes each semester and graduate sooner if you do not work. This may mean a few lean years struggling to make ends meet, however it will allow you to begin working in your chosen field sooner, with the financial benefits of a college degree.

A mature woman with a family who returns to school to continue her education is a good example of someone who may need to prioritize her work over school. While it is still important to continue investing in her education and working toward her degree, she would likely need to put work considerations first because her work supports the family.

Another reason to begin working sooner rather than later is that it allows you to begin saving for retirement. It is never too early to begin saving for retirement, and a retirement account is one of the most important savings vehicles to invest in. The preference is to save in an employer-sponsored retirement savings plan such as a 401k or 403b if available. A 401k is a traditional employer sponsored retirement account and a 403b is for employees of tax-exempt organizations, such as public schools, universities, and non-profits. Check to see if one of these options is available to you. If so, take full advantage of it, by saving as soon as possible.

Retirement savings plans are one of the more lucrative savings vehicles you can invest in for a few reasons. First, and most importantly, a 401k or 403b typically earns a company match whereby the company you work for matches a certain percentage of the deposits you make into the account. As an example, a company might contribute a 50 percent match up to 6 percent of your pre-tax earnings or a 100 percent match up to 4 percent of your pre-tax earnings. The match is super-important because it is the equivalent of *free money*. This may be the only time when you will get free money from anyone, so take advantage!

Let's take an example. If you earn $25,000 per year and your company has a 401k plan that provides a 50 percent match up to 6 percent of your pre-tax earnings, for every dollar you invest in the company's retirement plan, the company will invest $.50 in the plan for you, up to 6 percent of your salary. For every dollar you save, you will essentially be earning at least $.50 interest. That is a 50 percent return on your investment! You will not get a guaranteed 50 percent rate of return on any other savings account or investment account. Ladies, the 401K is something we should be excited about!

Let's suppose you contribute 6% of your pre-tax salary so that you can take full advantage of the free money match your company is offering. Over the course of one year, you will have contributed $1,500 ($25,000 x .06), which is great! But the best part is that you will also receive $750 from the company match, so instead of $1,500 you will have $2250 in your retirement account by the end of the year. Now that is pretty special. And this figure represents the contribution alone, before your account has earned any interest.

To top it off, 401k contributions are pre-tax contributions. Therefore the money that you save and your employer contributes is not considered taxable earnings, so you pay no federal income tax on this money until you retire. This tax benefit can add huge savings to your nest egg, especially as your salary increases over time. The goal with a 401k account is to save over the long-term for retirement, so the money you invest today will continue to grow until you withdraw it during retirement.

Every plan has specific guidelines and rules, so it is important to research your plan and understand the rules and benefits. Some plans let you borrow against your savings, while others may not. Some also have more investment options than others. You *always* want to check with the plan's administrator or the company that monitors and invests the funds to determine the rules and benefits for your specific plan.

## Strategic Step No. 5: Invest to Capitalize on Compound Interest

Compound interest is interest earned on both the initial principal and the interest that has accumulated in the account. Ladies, please understand that compound interest is a *beautiful* mechanism for enabling our money to grow more quickly over time. Many types of investments, including 401K accounts and mutual funds, compound the interest paid. Let's look at an example to understand how it can really help us become wealthy.

Let's say you decide to begin investing $50 into a mutual fund each month. You decide to invest this monthly amount no matter what other expenses or bills you have and you're pretty confident that you can do it because this figure is what you routinely spend on leisure activities like dinner with friends or shopping. You do the research and find a mutual fund that has produced an annual rate of return of 12 percent over the past ten years. Some years the rate of return has been higher and some years lower, but on average the return is 12 percent. You begin investing in this mutual fund when you are twenty-years old and continue investing $50 per month for the next twenty years. How much money would the account have accumulated at the end of the twenty years if it continues earning 12 percent per year?

Before we reveal how much money will be in your account, let's compare a few other options. Option one would be if you had continued spending the $50 per month on leisure activities. What would the net savings have been? Well, that's simple, exactly nothing. No money would have been saved.

A second option would be to deposit the $50 per month into a traditional savings account which currently earns less than 1 percent interest, let's say .75 percent interest. Calculating how much you would have deposited into the account $50 x 12 months x 20 years = $600 per year x 20 years = $12,000 that you will deposit into the account over the course of twenty years. In addition to the money you deposited, the account will earn another $1,005 in interest over twenty years, totaling $13,005.

Let's compare the savings account option to the mutual fund with an average rate of return of 12 percent. The monthly deposits of $50 over twenty years are the same--$50 x 12 months x 20 years = $12,000 in deposits. However, instead of earning the .75 percent interest you would get in a traditional savings account, you are now earning 12 percent interest annually which will result in a total account balance of $46,475 at the end of twenty years. If that does not convince you of the benefits of investing to get the full benefit of compound interest, I don't know what would.

The way that compound interest works is the first year you would earn 12 percent interest on only on the original $600 deposit. By the second year you'd earn 12 percent interest on $694 or the value of your first year's deposits and the interest earned on the second year's deposits. By the third year, the interest would be on the first two years' deposits and interest, plus the third year's deposits, and so on. The original deposit of $600 continues to earn interest for nineteen more years! Likewise, the interest earned on that first $600 continues to earn interest for nineteen years. This is the powerful benefit of compound interest and this is the reason we should be excited about investing to benefit from it.

For those who do not have an employer-sponsored retirement plan, consider opening a Roth IRA or a traditional IRA for yourself. You will unfortunately not have the benefit of "free money match", but your savings will still benefit from the higher rate of compound interest and the tax benefits of retirement savings.

### *Strategic Step No. 6: Avoid Buying on Credit*

Purchasing on credit means that you are borrowing money to make a purchase. Of course, financial institutions are not lending you money out of the kindness of their hearts, but because they want to collect interest on the loan. Using a credit card to purchase clothes and groceries or to go on vacation, is essentially the same as borrowing money to make these purchases. If you consider the interest rates that many credit-card companies charge, it is simply unwise to borrow and pay interest for a new pair of shoes or enjoying a night out with friends. So the next time you're faced with making a purchase on credit, think about whether it's worth borrowing the money and paying interest to make the purchase. Instead of charging, begin paying for your purchases with cash or a debit card.

### Strategic Step No. 7: Pay Down Credit-Card Debt

Credit card debt is a money drain that should be avoided whenever possible. If you are paying 12 to 18 percent interest on a credit card, the interest charges are a giant hit on your finances and you may not even notice them. Remember the compound interest we discussed? Well compound interest also applies to credit cards, except in this case, you are paying the compound interest instead of receiving it.

To put it pointedly, having credit-card debt is the equivalent of paying the type of interest rates you could be *earning* on your money by investing instead of spending. If you are serious about building a nest egg and creating wealth for yourself, it is critical to immediately stop using credit for anything but large, essential items. Big ticket items like a home, car, or large purchases you need for your home are really the only things to consider financing. Notice I said need for your home, not want for your home. Furniture is a need, but expensive furniture is a want. On the other hand, if your refrigerator breaks and you need a new one, then yes that would qualify as a need and would be worth paying for with a credit card. Of course, if there is a way to anticipate that your old fridge is nearing the end of its lifespan, you can save up for this expense in advance. Even paying a portion of the cost with cash and financing the rest may be preferable to financing the entire purchase.

## *Strategic Step No. 8: Buy a Home as Soon as You Can Afford to*

Buying a home is no small task. There are many steps involved and for most of us it is the largest and most expensive purchase we ever make. Owning a home is a great opportunity and a great responsibility, therefore you'll want to consider carefully when the timing is right to purchase a home.

While buying a home is a big financial commitment, for most people the home is also one of their greatest sources of wealth. Purchasing a home allows you to begin building wealth at a much faster rate because of the significant tax benefits, equity and appreciation that come with homeownership. Homeowners acquire wealth at a much higher and faster rate than non-homeowners.

***Strategic Step No 9: Understand the Financial Impact of Marriage***

In addition to marriage being a commitment to honor and care for your spouse, it is also a legal contract. Marriage is a legal commitment to be partners, and there are substantial legal and financial considerations that come along with it. As we discussed in Chapter Two, Black Americans marry at a lower rate than other races, which has an impact on our finances.

I want to be careful how I state this, because I do not recommend that anyone marry strictly for financial reasons. However, we ladies have to be aware of the financial implications of our decisions regarding marriage. For example, are you saving up for a dream wedding that will cost tens of thousands of dollars before you have purchased your first home together? Consider the impact this debt will have on your new marriage and ask if it is worth it. Are you and your partner in a long-term committed relationship that brings all the duties of husband and wife, but none of the financial benefits and legal protections of marriage? Closely consider the impact these additional benefits could have on your finances. Would it mean the ability to share health insurance benefits, purchase a home together and receive spousal retirement benefits?

Again, I do not recommend marring for financial reasons; however, I do recommend learning about the financial and legal benefits and possible drawbacks of marriage to inform your decision. One last thing on the subject: remember, to not make a decision to marry is actually a decision.

## Strategic Step No. 10: Treat Your Time As If It Were Money

There is a quote attributed to Mark Twain that says, "Buy land, they're not making any more of it." I love this saying because it truly expresses the importance of investing in land and real estate. I would take this thinking a step further and say that before you have accumulated enough money to invest in land or real estate, you can begin investing time wisely. Since there is no waiting period, we can immediately begin spending our time more wisely.

Think about this: Regardless of how much money we have, we each have exactly twenty-four hours in a day; no more and no less. No amount of money can buy us more time. Therefore, you could say that time is more valuable than money. If we are serious about building wealth, we must begin to use a part of every day to cultivate and grow our money. This sounds time-consuming, but it really isn't and I'll tell you why.

Each day we are blessed with twenty-four hours to use before our time bank is replenished. No matter what we do, we cannot get back yesterday and tomorrow is not promised. The way that we decide to use our gift of time is an indicator of how successful we will be and how likely we are to acquire wealth. We cannot build wealth if we do not use our time wisely, because if we are wasteful with our time, we're likely to be wasteful with our money. Since wealth takes time to accumulate, wasting time limits our ability to grow wealth.

Using our time strategically, we benefit more in the long run and have more to show for our efforts. Being strategic about time doesn't mean that we should try to fill each day with as much as we can. Rather, it simply means thinking about the things that are most important to get done that day and working to accomplish those few tasks.

Using time strategically also means we should not let other people use our time unwisely. Our time is too valuable to let others waste it. Treating our time as we treat our money means we will not give it so freely to people and things that are not worthy. If you know people who waste a lot of their own time, chances are they are going to try to waste your time also. Pay attention to these time wasters and take action not to let them waste your time.

One final tip for saving time is to learn to do things fast. While it is important to learn to do things correctly, especially important things, not all things have to be done perfectly. Using time efficiently sometimes means completing a task in the best way that you can within a designated timeframe. If it is not an important task, then there is no need to worry about doing it perfectly. Use your judgment to determine things that need to be done very well compared to things that simply need to get done. Often, getting things done is more important than having a perfectly finished product every time.

Trying to complete a task perfectly can sometimes lead to procrastination or starting and not finishing. It's better to use our time to do the task, not worry about how to do it perfectly. After all, most things do not need to be done perfectly; they simply need to be finished.

***Strategic Step No. 11: Sharpen Your Communication Skills***

Communication is a vital part of life and today we have more ways to communicate than ever before. If you think about it, just two decades ago, if you wanted to communicate with someone, you could call them on the phone, mail a letter, send a fax, or go speak with them in person. Today, in addition to those ways of getting in touch with someone, we can also email, instant message (IM), text, video chat or FaceTime® or message them through a variety of social media outlets. Along with these new ways to communicate, there has been a shift in communication styles and in what is considered acceptable and appropriate communication and expression.

In addition to more ways to communicate, the Internet has also given us access to an abundance of information. The availability of so much information at our fingertips brings great benefits long with, an increased expectation to know how to access and communicate the information. Most jobs require use of computer technology in some fashion. Many trade professions and technical jobs that were once manual now use computerized diagnostic and repair tools. Learning to use a computer is no longer an option; it is a necessity.

A key step in building wealth is to be able to increase our earnings by getting a good job. I define a good job as one that pays well, pays consistently, has prospects for career or entrepreneurial advancement, and is reliable enough to allow long-term financial planning. In order to compete for and obtain a good job, you must be able to communicate effectively.

Even before you are interviewed and hired, you will need to have a well-written resume or job application.

The higher you climb in education and career, the higher the expectations that you have the skills to communicate effectively in speaking, writing, listening, and interpreting information. I recommend developing the following communication skills over time as you continue on your path to building wealth.

***Improve your computer skills.*** Computer skills are an essential part of almost any job function now. If you will be working in a field of study that uses your college degree, chances are high that you will need at least a working knowledge of Microsoft Word®, Excel®, and Power Point®. Depending on the type of job you have, you may also need to learn other programs such as Microsoft Project®, Access® or Publisher®.

***Learn to type.*** Gone are the days of old where people typed on a typewriter or word processor. Personal computers (or PCs) are ubiquitous now, and typing skills are more necessary than ever before. It used to be that typing was a skill needed only by secretaries or writers, but these days, typing is a skill that everyone can benefit from.

Learning to type fast will save time in searching the Internet, typing papers for school and projects for work. It will also save you time in creating documents such as spreadsheets, slide presentations, and so forth. There are many typing tutorial software and games that allow you to practice and improve your speed and accuracy. I recommend learning to type as soon as possible because this skill will begin saving you time immediately.

**_Build a better vocabulary_.** As mentioned previously, today we communicate by writing more than ever before in the form of emails, texting, and instant messaging. Building an extensive vocabulary will enable you to choose the best word to communicate the meaning you want to convey. An extensive vocabulary is priceless in helping written communications flourish. One of the best ways to improve your vocabulary and written communication is to read and listen to others who communicate well. I recommend listening to public radio as one way to help improve your verbal communication and build a better vocabulary. Using a thesaurus and dictionary while writing are also effective ways to improve your vocabulary. People will respond better in business and personal affairs if you are able to articulate your thoughts with ease and confidence.

**Improve your writing skills**. Good writing is concise while effectively expressing the message. Unless you are writing a novel or other work of fiction, it's probably best to get to the point. To become more adept at writing professionally, consider investing in a style book to refer to over the course of your education and career.

Also consider investing in a good quality newspaper or professional journal of your choice to become familiar with concise professional writing. A few newspapers to consider are the *New York Times*, *The Wall Street Journal*, or *The Washington Post*. These newspapers also provide interesting and informative articles that are often written from a global perspective, so you will be increasing your awareness of global issues as well. Journals such as *National*

*Geographic* and *The Economist* are extremely well-written and serve this purpose as well.

***Improve your listening skills.*** Listening is one of the most critical success skills a person can develop. Good listening requires at least three steps: hearing what is being communicated; second, interpreting the message within the context of what is already known; and finally, understanding and communicating your understanding back to the speaker.

Developing good listening skills and good listening etiquette improves our professional communications and interactions in our personal life, the classroom, and the workplace. Being a good listener and communicator will help you to advance as a student and in your profession

***Improve your presentation skills.*** Presentation skills are essential in high school, college and in many job functions. A presentation can range from a formal report or PowerPoint to effectively communicating ideas during class, a client meeting or on a job interview. Many job functions also require presenting information to teams, clients or managers. There are a host of books to help improve presentation skills and since these skills are in such high demand in many industries, the investment will continue to pay off for many years to come.

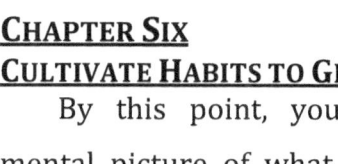

## CHAPTER SIX
### CULTIVATE HABITS TO GROW WEALTH

By this point, you should have a mental picture of what it takes to build wealth from scratch and understand that building wealth is a lifelong process, not something that can be achieved overnight. Building lasting wealth does not have to be a dream or fantasy. It is a goal that we can reach by practicing good financial habits over time. These habits include exercising discipline to ear, save and invest our money.

Habits are most effective when practiced consistently so that they become part of our daily or weekly routines. The more often we practice a habit, the faster it becomes part of our routine and the better we become at it. Establishing wealth habits is no different. To increase our chance of success, we can implement small daily and weekly habits to incorporate in our lifestyle easily so the change is not overwhelming. With few exceptions, individuals who obtain wealth in one generation are able to do so by careful planning in their daily lives. Following is a list of wealth habits that, if practiced routinely, will begin to impact your finances. Incorporate these habits slowly into your daily, weekly, and monthly routine, and in time they will become second nature.

Although it may be tempting to dive headfirst and try to implement all the habits at once, that is probably not practical and may be taking on too much at one time. Start slowly and give yourself time to master one or two habits before adding on a new one. Remember, the goal is to build wealth over time with careful and consistent planning, saving, and investing. Some of these habits you may already be practicing; if so, that is great! Give yourself credit for those right away and keep up the good work. Continue adding more good habits and curtailing the bad ones.

**Wealth Habit No. 1: Pay yourself first.** In his ground-breaking book by this title, Jesse B. Brown, an investment advisor, puts forth the idea that you are the most important person to pay with each paycheck you receive. He recommends saving 10 percent from each paycheck before you pay even a single bill or monthly expense. In my opinion, this underscores the value of the 401k as a savings tool. The 401k enables you to pay yourself before other expenses are paid.

The best part is that once you have set up the deductions through your company's 401k provider, the money will be taken out automatically. From that point on, the 401k is an effortless way to save money from each paycheck and benefit from a company match, which is the equivalent of getting free money. Other ways to pay yourself first would include setting up an automatic savings into an IRA or savings account.

**Wealth Habit No. 2: Begin Saving As Soon As You Can.** It is never too soon to begin planning and saving for the future. Although many recommend saving at least 10% of your gross salary, I know from experience that this amount may not always possible. However if you cannot save 10% of your gross income, try to at least save something. Even 1 to 2 percent is better than nothing.

While it would be nice to put away 10 percent of your gross salary, there are times when you may be on a shoestring budget and there is really nowhere to pull from. If that's the case, try to think about ways to earn extra money. Maybe you can take on a part-time job to get over the hump and help you to save up a small emergency fund. It's typically recommended that you save three to six months' worth of expenses in an emergency savings fund for unexpected events like losing a job or a personal injury. It may seem daunting to save this amount if your budget is already tight, but you don't have to do it all at once. It's okay to take small steps to reach your goal.

**Wealth Habit No. 3: Track Your Spending and Know Where Every Dollar Goes.** It is extremely important to track spending to know exactly where your hard-earned money is going. Saving receipts or jotting down your expenses in a notebook are good habits to develop. Also reviewing and tracking your monthly bills and other expenses. By tracking your spending, you may notice spending traps you were not aware of, such as eating out too often, unnecessary shopping, three-dollar coffee drinks, and entertainment costs. A big culprit is the "hidden" bank fees that we do not always notice on our statements. These are fees charged by credit-card companies and banks for things such as late payments, failure to maintain a minimum balance in a checking account, bounced checks, and processing charges for paying a bill online or by phone. These hidden costs may not be apparent until you start to write them down every month.

One quick way to track your expenses is to use a specific debit card in lieu of cash for all purchases. The end of the month, you can record the purchases through your bank statement. This can also be a way to track your monthly household bills and other expenses. I have found it helpful to write my expenses in a notebook each month. The practice allows me to notice when bills are paid late or if a payment was missed. I also notice if my bills begin to increase from month to month. For example when signing up for a special promotion for cable or cell phone and after the promotion ends, the bill increases, often without warning. By tracking these expenses on a monthly basis, I can catch the increase right away and decide if I want to keep the service, cancel or change it.

**Wealth Habit No 4: Teach your children the value of money.** We all want what's best for our children and yet there are only so many hours in a day and so much time available to impart the wisdom and life lessons we would like to share. It can be challenging to find time to discuss with our children the importance of earning money, saving, and investing. But if you think about it, teaching our kids about money is a gift that will help equip them with financial independence and financial security their entire lives.

There is no doubt that learning about money and getting a financial education early in life allows our children to hold onto more of their hard-earned money down the road. In my own life, it has been important for me to learn about finances so that I can teach my three daughters the value of money. I also wanted them to understand that money is important because it allows you to do the things you want to do, not for selfish reasons or greed, but because it helps you to take care of your family, help friends and relatives, support charitable causes, and give back to the community. We can start teaching our children the value of money by giving them an allowance or allowing them to earn money by doing extra chores. We can also encourage them to do chores for neighbors who are sick or elderly. Encouraging our children, particularly our boys to go to the store, shovel snow, mow lawns or take out trash for a neighbor who does not have a man in the house, is a good way to instill a sense of responsibility and pride of helping others.

Our daughters can also be encouraged to help sick or elderly neighbors in need by helping with light meal preparation, laundry, light cleaning and tidying. Often seniors have family members that are willing to pay a young person to help their loved one because they do not have the time to do it themselves. As parents we can facilitate working through a daily or weekly rate for services our children provide.

When I was about 12 years old, I used to sit with an elderly neighbor for $5 per day. I prepared his cereal, made the bed washed the dishes and lightly cleaned the kitchen after his breakfast and lunch and sat and watched television with him. I cannot tell you what a good learning experience this was for me. It helped me to be more responsible and I loved earning my own money. From then on I was hooked, and I always looked for other opportunities to earn money during summer vacation. Earning their own money from a young age will help teach our children the value of the dollar as well as responsibility

**Wealth Habit No. 5: Invest in continuing education and training for yourself and your family.** Children follow our example and believe what they see over what they are told. If we want our children to invest in their education and their future, we have to show them the importance of education by "talking the talk and walking the walk." When our children see us invest time and money in education and continuous learning, they begin to think of learning and studying as high-value activities.

Purchasing books, going to the local library, subscribing to magazines and newspapers, watching educational TV programming, taking continuing education courses, going back to school to advance our education, taking training and seminars are all ways we can practice lifelong learning. For our children we may invest in supplemental workbooks and learning materials, tutoring services, and test preparation courses. Foreign language courses, and lessons in, art, music, dance or sports are all great ways to supplements our children's' learning experiences outside of school.

**Wealth Habit No. 6: Be an entrepreneur.** Owning a business is one of the fastest ways to accumulate wealth. Think about the people in our society who are the most successful financially. They are typically entrepreneurs. Even the most successful entertainers and athletes tend to build their fortune by doing endorsements and licensing deals. Theoretically, entrepreneurship enables us to earn unlimited amounts of passive income. Entrepreneurs are able to employ others to work for them and thereby benefit from their own work as well as the work of their employees.

Entrepreneurs also serve society. They not only provide a product or service that people need or want, they also create jobs. If you think about it, being an entrepreneur is a great way to give back to our community and to society. Give some thought to different ways you can go into business for yourself. If you don't naturally feel like an entrepreneur, don't worry, just think a little about what you really enjoy doing and then picture yourself doing that every day and making money from it. It's really that simple. Business ideas are everywhere around us, and the best business for us is often incorporating something we have a natural talent or leaning toward.

**Wealth Habit No. 7: *Learn to invest your own money.*** No matter how much or how little money you have, it will be important to develop an understanding of your own financial situation so that you can assess where you are currently, where you would like to be in the future, and how you can get there. Just as it is important to take ownership of your health or your household, for example, it is equally important to be in charge of your finances. Remember the example of the lottery winner who has not gained the financial knowledge and understanding to make sound financial choices and therefore ends up broke. While consulting with financial professionals for advice and guidance can be a good idea, it should be just that—*consulting*. The decisions are ultimately your own to make. And only you (and your spouse and beneficiaries) have to live with the impact of your financial decisions. Therefore, it's important to learn as much as you can about investing and put that knowledge to good use.

The easiest way to get your feet wet, learning about investing is to begin with reading simple investment books, magazines and watching financial programs on television. This will provide an initial entrance into the world of finance and investing.

**Wealth Habit No. 8: Surround yourself with people who share your values of God, family, education, time, money and entrepreneurship.** Surrounding ourselves with others who share similar values and goals is important to our success. Growing up, my mother always stressed to my brother and me the importance of our association. She instilled in us that you pick up the habits of the people you surround yourself with and become like them. Even if you do not develop the same character traits, chances are other people will begin to believe that you share the same traits, whether negative or positive.

Like attracts like, and people tend to associate with others who are like them. There is a saying that "a person is the sum of their five closest friends." I don't know if that is true, but I do know being around positive-minded people can't help but rub off in a good way.

**Wealth Habit No. 9: Invest in items that appreciate and limit spending on Items that depreciate.** In the iconic movie *Baby Boy*, starring Tyrese Gibson as Jody and Ving Rhames as Melvin; Melvin gives Jody a quick lesson on investing. Melvin explains the difference between "guns" and "butter," arguing that figuratively "guns" are assets or things that appreciate in value, such as real estate, stocks, bonds, and artwork. These things typically gain in value over time. "Butter," on the other hand," refers to items that depreciate and lose value after you purchase them, such as cars, clothes, and jewelry. The distinction between guns and butter has been around a long time often in political discussions, but for many of my generation, this speech served as an introduction to purchasing assets versus items that depreciate. We should take Melvin's advice and spend more on the appreciating "guns" and less on the depreciating "butter" that makes us look and feel good, but has no lasting monetary value.

***Wealth Habit No. 10: Hold on to your money.*** Remember money is power, and she who holds the money holds the power. Once you spend your money, you have given away your power. Put another way, money is leverage, and the person who has the money has the leverage.

Leverage can be defined many ways, including the power to act effectively or the ability to do more with a similar amount of something.

The longer you hold onto your money, the more it will grow and the more power or leverage you will have. One way to think about leverage is a way to do more with the resources you have. Growing your money into a large pool of wealth, will enable you to have a much greater impact

**Wealth Habit No. 11: Value money above material things.** In my opinion it is okay to place a high value on money, but *not* on material things. Again, this is only my opinion, but from a practical standpoint, material items are only valuable in the sense that they fill a practical need. Therefore, a shoe is only valuable as it protects and supports your foot.

A $500 designer shoe is not inherently more valuable than a $35 bargain shoe.

Can you imagine spending $1,500 on a designer purse? I hope that your answer is heck no! I cannot imagine spending that kind of money on a purse. Here's why: If you took $1,500 and invested it in a mutual fund yielding an average of 12 percent annually, after twenty years you would have nearly $15,000 just from that initial $1500 investment. If you let the funds accumulate for thirty years, you would have a whopping $45,000! So I ask you to be the judge, which would you rather have in thirty years—$45,000 or an old purse?

**Wealth Habit No. 12: Teach others about saving and investing.** I believe one of our greatest strengths as women is our ability to network and share information. As we become more financially savvy, it will benefit our communities even more if we can teach others in our circles—our spouses, partners, parents, children, siblings, aunts, uncles cousins nieces, nephews and neighbors, —the importance of saving and investing to build wealth. Learn as much as you can and then pass along the information and resources to others. Sharing what we have learned with others not only motivates and encourages them, but also serves to reinforce our own knowledge and understanding. As the saying goes, "experience is the best teacher," so share your personal experiences as you begin to learn and experiment with saving and investing. Together we can be the catalyst to start a movement and get more of our sisters and brothers saving and investing in the future. Remember each one teach one!

## AFTERWARD

Thank you for purchasing the Black Girl's Guide to Building Wealth. I hope you have enjoyed reading this book and that you find the information practical and useful. My wish is that each reader learns at least a few helpful practices to help her increase her potential to earn, save and invest with confidence. If you would like to learn more or continue the dialogue on wealth-building, please email me: lakisharodwellgreen@gmail.com. I look forward to receiving your questions, comments and suggestions. Also visit my website BlackGirlsGetMoney.com for useful resources and to register for a **Black Girl's Guide Wealth Building Workshop** near you. I hope to see you there!

Until then,

Be healthy, be happy and be rich!

*Lakisha*

## APPENDIX

1. US Census Bureau Report: *Marital Status 2000*

2. US Census Bureau Report: *The Black Population With a Bachelor's Degree or Higher by Race and Hispanic Origin: 2006-2010*

3. US Census Bureau Report: *The Black Population 2010*

4. US Census Bureau Report: *The Big Payoff: Educational Attainment and Synthetic Estimates of Work Life Earnings*

5. US Census Bureau Report: *Home Values 2000*

6. US Census Bureau Report: *Marital Events of Americans 2009*

7. **Sports Illustrated**: *How (and Why) Athletes Go Broke* by Pablo S. Torre

8. *The Demographics of Wealth essay series by the Federal Reserve Bank of St. Louis* by Ray Boshara, William Emmons and Brian Noeth

9. *Historical Marriage Trends from 1890-2010 A Focus on Race Differences* by Diana B. Elliott, Kristy Krivickas and Matthew W. Brault, US Census Bureau

10. *The Racial Wealth Gap: Why Policy Matters* by Laura Sullivan, Tatijana Meschede, Lars Dietrich and Thomas Shapiro – Institute for Assets and Social Policy, Brandeis University and Amy Traub, Catherine Ruetschlin and Tamara Draut- Demos

11. US Census Bureau Report: *Income and Poverty in the United States 2014*

12. *Major Decisions: What Graduates Earn Over Their Lifetimes* by Brad Hershbein and Melissa Kearney- The Hamilton Project

13. *The Millionaire Next Door: The Surprising Secrets of America's Wealthy* by Thomas J. Stanley and William D. Danko

14. *Pay Yourself First: The African American Guide to Financial Success and Security* by Jesse B. Brown

15. *Surprising Statistics About Small Businesses* by Jason Nazar,

## Notes

## NOTES

## ABOUT THE AUTHOR

Lakisha Rodwell-Green is a self-published author whose aim is to increase awareness about social and economic issues affecting the African American community, particularly women, children, families and those impacted by poverty. Mrs. Rodwell Green is the owner of Kisha Rose Skincare, a boutique skin and hair care company specializing in problem skin and hair. After earning dual degree from Temple University in biology and Spanish she has worked in pharmaceutical research for the past twenty years. She grew up in Philadelphia, Pennsylvania and currently lives in suburban Philadelphia with her husband and their three daughters.

www.ingramcontent.com/pod-product-compliance
Lightning Source LLC
Chambersburg PA
CBHW021435170526
45164CB00001B/249